DUE DATE

JAN 20	DEC 11		
JAN 28	MAR 05		
FEB 25	FEB 22		
MAR 05			
MAY 28			
NOV 03			
DEC 09			
APR 28	DISCARD		
MAY 18			
OCT 11			
OCT 24			
JAN 10			
MAY 17			
OCT 16			
OCT 24			
MAY 22			
NOV 20			
			Printed in USA

THE Arrow AND THE Lamp

The Story of Psyche

Retold by Margaret Hodges
Illustrated by Donna Diamond

Little, Brown and Company
Boston   Toronto   London

First Edition

The story of Psyche and Eros was written in the second century A.D. by Lucius Apuleius.
It is found in his Latin novel, *The Metamorphoses*, also called *The Golden Ass*.

Library of Congress Cataloging-in-Publication Data
Hodges, Margaret.
  The arrow and the lamp.

  Summary: Relates how Psyche married the god of love, Eros, lost him, and had to
overcome many obstacles before she became an immortal and could join him on
Mount Olympus.
  1. Psyche (Greek deity)—Juvenile literature. 2. Eros (Greek deity)—Juvenile literature. 3. Aphrodite (Greek deity)—Juvenile literature. [1. Psyche (Greek deity) 2. Eros
(Greek deity) 3. Aphrodite (Greek deity) 4. Mythology, Greek] I. Diamond, Donna, ill.
II. Apuleius. Metamorphoses. III. Title. BL820.P8.H63 1987   292'.211
86-2728   ISBN 0-316-36790-7

10 9 8 7 6 5 4 3 2 1

NIL

*Published simultaneously in Canada
by Little, Brown & Company (Canada) Limited*

Printed in Italy

To Joseph Campbell for his *Myths to Live By*

*"The Greeks. . . regarded Eros, the god of love,
as the eldest of the gods; but also as the youngest,
born fresh and dewy-eyed in every loving heart."*

M. H.

On the Greek island of Rhodes is "the valley of the butter-flies." Every summer, countless thousands of butterflies settle there on the leaves of the trees. When they are disturbed, they fly up in a golden cloud, and the Greeks say that each butterfly is a soul, like Psyche. This is her story.

The Characters in the Story

Psyche (*Sī′kē*)
meaning the Mind, the Soul, or the Self.

Aphrodite (*Af ro dī′tē*)
called Venus in Roman myth; she is the goddess of love and beauty.

Eros (*E′ros*)
called Amor or Cupid in Roman myth; he is the son of Aphrodite and makes both gods and humans fall in love.

Persephone (*Per sef′o nē*)
called Proserpina in Roman myth; with Hades (*Hā′dēs*), her husband, she rules over the underground world of the dead, also called Hades, which is reached by crossing the river Styx (*Stix*). King Hades is Pluto in Roman myth.

Zeus (*Zūs*)
called Jupiter or Jove in Roman myth; he is "the father of light" and ruler of the gods, all of whom live on Mount Olympus. They drink nectar and eat ambrosia, which makes them immortal.

ONCE A KING AND A QUEEN had three daughters. All three were beautiful, but the youngest, Psyche, was different. Her sisters were content to know what they were told. Psyche always wanted to know more. She was so lovely that men called her a new Aphrodite, a young goddess of love and beauty, but no man dared to marry a goddess. So while the two older sisters found husbands and went away to live in their own homes, Psyche stayed on alone with her father and mother.

Now all might have been well if golden, sweet-smiling Aphrodite had not heard of Psyche. The goddess came up out of the sea to find out whether men were really leaving her temples empty and silent and throwing flowers in the streets where Psyche walked. And when Aphrodite saw that it was true, she no longer smiled. She was furious, and she said to herself, "This girl is mortal. Beautiful she may be, but like all mortals she will die, and until she dies, she must never have a happy day. I shall see to that."

Then she called her favorite child, Eros, and he came flying to her. This young god, as fair as his mother, had golden wings on which he moved swiftly and unseen on his mysterious errands, often doing mischief. He carried a golden bow and a quiver filled with arrows.

"Go to this girl, this Psyche," said Aphrodite. "Wound her with one of your arrows. Pour bitterness on her lips. Then find her the vilest husband in the world—mean, bad-tempered, ugly—and make her fall in love with him."

There were two springs of water in Aphrodite's garden—one bitter, the other sweet. Carrying water from both springs, Eros flew off, invisible.

He found Psyche asleep. Her beauty moved him to pity, but, obeying his mother's command, he poured bitter water on her lips and touched her side with one of his arrows. Psyche felt the pain and opened her eyes. She could not see Eros, but as he looked into her eyes, the arrow trembled in his hand, and by chance he wounded himself. He poured a little of the sweet water on her forehead, and flew away.

Still no lovers came to ask for Psyche's hand in marriage, so the king and the queen, guessing that

their daughter had somehow angered one of the gods, asked an oracle to look into the future and tell them what could be done to find a husband for her.

The oracle answered with frightening words: "Dress your daughter for her funeral. She will never marry a mortal man but will be the bride of a creature with wings, feared even by the gods. Take Psyche to the stony top of the mountain that looks down on your city, and leave her there alone to meet her fate."

When they heard this prophecy, all the people wept with Psyche's father and mother. But Psyche said, "Tears will not help me. I was doomed from the moment when you called me the new Aphrodite. It must be Aphrodite herself whom I have angered. Obey the oracle before the goddess punishes all of you. I alone must bear her anger."

Psyche led the way to the mountaintop and said good-bye to her weeping parents and the crowd of folk who had sadly followed her. When all were gone, she sat down, trembling and afraid, to wait. But no monster husband came. Instead, the warm west wind began to blow and, raising her gently in the air,

carried her down the far side of the mountain to a
green and flowering meadow in a hidden valley.

Psyche fell peacefully asleep in the soft grass.
When she woke, she saw a grove of tall trees watered
by a clear stream. In the grove stood a marvelous
palace, its golden pillars topped with a roof of carved
sandalwood and ivory.

She entered through the open doorway, wonder-
ing at the light that flashed from silver walls. Surely
only a god could have made such a palace! Psyche
passed from room to room, walking on floors made of
precious stones, until she came to a marble pool filled
with scented water.

Then a voice spoke to her: "Lady, all of this is yours. Ask for whatever you like." Unseen hands led her to the bath and afterward clothed her in a robe of fine silk. A table appeared, spread with delicious food, and Psyche ate and drank while invisible servants waited on her and the air was filled with the sound of sweet voices singing.

When darkness fell, Psyche found a bed ready for her and lay down to rest. But in the night she woke, feeling the presence of someone standing beside her bed, and she was full of fear. Then a voice said, "Do not be afraid, Psyche. I am the husband you have been waiting for. Trust me. No harm will come to you. Only do not try to see me." Psyche's husband stayed with her all night long, but before daylight he was gone.

For some months Psyche lived in the palace, surrounded by beauty and comfort. The unseen servants answered all her wishes and when her unseen husband came at night, he was always kind. She began to long for the sound of his voice and very soon fell deeply in love with him. Still, the days seemed empty and she often felt lonely.

One night her husband said to her, "Psyche, your sisters are looking for you. If you hear them calling, do not answer."

Psyche promised to obey, but she wished more and more to see a face. The clear waters of the pool reflected only her own face, and the palace now seemed like a prison. At last her husband found her weeping and, taking her in his arms, said, "Well, my love, have your wish, even if it brings trouble. The west wind shall carry your sisters here." And Psyche thanked him with grateful kisses.

The next day she heard her sisters calling to her from the mountaintop, and she called back to them. Then the west wind carried them down into the valley, and when they found Psyche safe and well, they embraced her joyfully. But their joy turned to

jealousy as she showed them her palace and they saw how she was dressed and waited on like a queen.

When Psyche confessed that she had never seen her husband, they spoiled her happiness by planting suspicions in her mind: "If your husband will not let you see him, he must be the monster that the oracle said you would marry. He is only biding his time until he is ready to kill you. Take our advice. The next time he comes, have a lamp and a sharp knife hidden at your side. When he is asleep, light the lamp and look at him. If he is a monster, kill him while there is yet time."

The west wind carried the sisters away as safely as they had come, but Psyche was tormented by what they had said. At last she filled a little lamp with oil and found a sharp knife, both of which she hid beside her bed.

That night, when her husband was asleep, she lit the lamp and saw him—not a monster, but the most beautiful of beings, a fair and graceful youth with golden wings, smiling even in his sleep. Psyche was moved by a deeper love than she had ever felt. She bent over her husband, and from the lamp, a drop of oil, burning hot, fell on his shoulder. Stung by the pain, he opened his eyes and looked at her

sternly. "Foolish Psyche," he said, "I knew how it would be. You could not trust me. You had to see for yourself. Now you will lose everything that I could give you, and I must lose you." Too late she knew who he was: Eros, the son of Aphrodite. There was a flash of golden wings and he was gone. The palace too was gone, and Psyche found herself alone again on the mountaintop.

Psyche was determined to find her lost husband, but although she walked all the roads of the world, she could not discover where he was. He had flown to one of his mother's many palaces, sick at heart and feverish with the burning pain of the oil from Psyche's lamp. Aphrodite was angrier than she had ever been. "You are meant to make mortals fall in love, not to fall in love yourself," she said. "However, you will soon be well and will forget all about that girl." She locked him into a chamber, and there he lay.

As Psyche searched for Eros, she came at last to a faraway river that flowed from a high waterfall. At the edge of the river stood a temple, and in its doorway she saw Aphrodite. She knelt at the feet of the goddess and begged Aphrodite to tell her where she could find Eros. But Aphrodite, jealous of her beauty, answered with a false smile, "I will give Eros back to you if you will do something for me." And when Psyche eagerly agreed, the goddess led her into the temple and showed her a room filled with a great heap of grains: corn and barley, poppy seed, lentils, and beans, all mixed together. "Anyone as ugly as you is fit only to work," Aphrodite said, scornfully. "Sort all of these grains into separate piles, and have it done by evening."

When the goddess had left her, Psyche sat down and began to cry. The task was impossible. But as she sat there weeping, she saw a procession of little ants coming out of the earth and running to her rescue. They attacked the heap of grains and carried each kind to a separate pile, never stopping until the work was done. Then they vanished into the earth.

When Aphrodite returned in the evening, she found Psyche sitting with folded hands. All the work was finished. "You do not deceive me, wretched girl," cried the goddess. "Someone has helped you. Tomorrow you must work alone, but your task is easy. Across the river is a field where golden sheep are grazing. Bring me a strand of their fleece."

At dawn Psyche went to the river and stepped into the water. But as she did so, she heard the whispering of the reeds that grew along the shore: "Psyche, the sheep are wild rams, as fierce as the sun's rays. They will batter you with their stony foreheads and pierce you with their sharp horns."

Psyche was ready to sink down into the river,

despairing. But the reeds whispered, "Do not give up.
Be patient. Things will change. Wait until the sun
sinks. Then the rams sleep, and you can easily gather
a strand of their golden fleece from the bushes along
the edge of the field." Psyche obeyed, and in the
evening gave the shining fleece to Aphrodite.

The goddess was enraged. She could not bear to
find Psyche still alive. "Tomorrow you must work
again," she said. She gave Psyche a crystal jar and
pointed to the waterfall that plunged from the mountain peak. "That is where the river Styx comes from
Hades, the land of death. Bring me water from the
top of the waterfall," she ordered. She thought to
herself, "The girl will never return. It is a just punish-
ment for stealing my son's love."

Psyche made her way to the foot of the mountain and climbed the steep and rugged path—up, up, on and on, fearing every moment that she would fall and be dashed to pieces. At last she reached the topmost crag, a rough and slippery rock, and saw that the torrent of water poured out of a cavern guarded by dragons with unwinking eyes. Psyche heard the waters roaring, "Beware!" and stood as if turned to stone by fear. Then, from high in the air above her,

there flew down an eagle, the messenger of Zeus, king of the gods. The eagle took the crystal jar in its claws and swooped past the dragons. It hovered at the top of the waterfall until the jar was filled to the brim, then brought it back to Psyche.

That night Aphrodite could hardly believe her eyes when she saw Psyche alive and well, bearing the jar of water in her hands. "I have obeyed all your commands," said Psyche. "I beg you to give me my husband."

"I have only one more task for you," said Aphrodite with a bitter smile. "If you accomplish this, Eros shall be yours forever. Go to the world of the dead and ask Queen Persephone to fill this box with some of her beauty." "For," she thought to herself, "no mortal comes back from Hades."

Psyche took the box. She knew now that Aphrodite wished nothing less than her death, and she climbed a high tower, ready to leap to the ground and so be taken at once to the land of the dead, never to return. But as she looked out from the top of the windy tower, a voice echoed from its walls: "Psyche, do not lose hope. There is a way to accomplish the last of your labors. Near at hand you will find a cave. A path leads through it to the river Styx. Carry two coins in your mouth to pay the ferryman who will row you across the river to Hades and back again. A three-headed dog guards the palace of Hades. Take two barley cakes for the dog. Give him one when you enter, the other when you leave."

Psyche found the cave and followed the dark path that led through it into the secret places of the earth. When she came to the river Styx, the ferryman took one of the coins from her mouth and rowed her across. When the fierce three-headed dog of Hades barked at her, she silenced him with a barley cake and went on to the jeweled palace of Hades. There Queen Persephone came to greet her. And when Psyche saw that gentle face, she knew why even Aphrodite wanted to have some of its beauty. The goddess took the box and put something into it,

saying in a voice both soft and kind, "Do not open this, my child. It is not for you."

Gratefully, Psyche took the box and ran from the palace. She gave her last cake to the three-headed dog, her last coin to the ferryman, and hurried up the path. But as she stepped out under the open sky, she thought, "My husband once said that I was beautiful. He may no longer think so, after all my labors. Perhaps I should keep a little of Persephone's beauty for myself." She opened the box. At once a deep sleep came over her, and she lay as if dead.

But even from afar, Eros saw her. He had recovered from his hurt, and his love for her was so strong that he burst open the locked door of his chamber and flew to her, tenderly wiping away the spell of sleep. He closed the box and gave it back to her. Then, with Psyche in his arms, he flew upward. As they neared the top of Mount Olympus the heavenly radiance shone brighter and brighter and in the

center of the light Psyche saw Zeus, the father of light. He called Aphrodite and all the other gods and goddesses together and spoke to them: "See this mortal girl whom Eros loves. No mortal can have Persephone's beauty, but Psyche has brought some of that beauty to us. So give her the food and drink of gods, and let her be one of us, never to die, never to be separated again from her love."

Finally, even Aphrodite said it should be so. Then from Psyche's shoulders delicate wings, like those of a butterfly, unfolded. And mortals, seeing butterflies in summer fields, remember Psyche and her love.